This book belongs to

_____

Michelle Obama

By Mary Nhin

Illustrated By
Yuliia Zolotova

This book is dedicated to my children –
Mikey, Kobe, and Jojo.

As a child, I watched my father suffer from a severe disease called multiple sclerosis.

This made me want to help out my family as much as possible by working hard and doing good at school.

My efforts were rewarded when I was chosen to be in a gifted class at school. When I got to high school, I went to a school for children who loved learning. It took us three hours round trip, but it was worth it!

I remember getting a lot of criticism even though I was dedicated and hard-working. People would often dismiss or not ask for my opinions simply because I was a girl. My teachers even tried to discourage me from applying to the college of my choice. They warned me that I was reaching too high.

That didn't stop me. I was determined to continue my education. I believed in myself, whether they believed in me or not.

I not only attended the college of my choice, Princeton University, I ended up graduating in the top tier of my class. Throughout my college years, I experienced discrimination and social alienation like never before.

Because of this, my heart called on me to help other minority students just like me. This led me to get involved with an organization which allowed me to work directly with children.

After I graduated from Princeton University, I continued my education by getting my law degree from Harvard University.

I found work at a law firm and was asked to mentor a new associate named Barack Obama.

Barack and I shared many things in common like social justice and helping those who are underrepresented. I married him and we had two daughters.

When he decided to run for President, I stood by his side and helped him campaign.

When he won, we made history and I became the first Black First Lady of the United States.

After we moved into the White House, I continued work as an advocate for poverty awareness, education, and health.

I started a campaign to provide healthier lunches to children. The Healthy, Hunger-Free Kids Act changed nutrition standards for schools by requiring that we serve more fruits, vegetables, whole grains, and fat-free and/or low-fat milk.

Being an African American woman, people have frequently underestimated me throughout my life but defying them has given me experiences that I've used to strengthen my career and the role I play in my community. I encourage you to do the same with your own challenges in life. They make us so much stronger. And when the time comes, pay it forward and help others who need it.

You should never view your challenges as a disadvantage. Instead, it's important for you to understand that your experience facing and overcoming adversity is actually one of your biggest advantages.

Timeline

1988 – Michelle graduates from Harvard Law School

2009 – Michelle becomes First Lady

2010 – Michelle launches *Let's Move*, an initiative to reverse the trend of childhood obesity

2012 – Michelle and her husband are awarded the Jerald Washington Memorial Founders' Award

2018 – Michelle releases *Becoming*, a memoir

2020 – Michelle wins a Grammy for her spoken word album

minimovers.tv

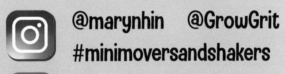 @marynhin   @GrowGrit
#minimoversandshakers

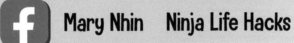 Mary Nhin   Ninja Life Hacks

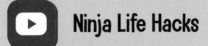 Ninja Life Hacks

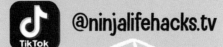 @ninjalifehacks.tv

Printed in Great Britain
by Amazon